C000227565

EFFIN' BIRDS

EFFIN' BIRDS

A Field Guide to Identification

FACK

Aaron Reynolds

unbound

First published in 2019

Unbound
6th Floor Mutual House, 70 Conduit Street, London W1S 2GF
www.unbound.com

All rights reserved

© Aaron Reynolds, 2019

The right of Aaron Reynolds to be identified as the author of
this work has been asserted in accordance with Section 77
of the Copyright, Designs and Patents Act 1988. No part
of this publication may be copied, reproduced, stored in a
retrieval system, or transmitted, in any form or by any means,
without the prior permission of the publisher, nor be otherwise
circulated in any form of binding or cover other than that in
which it is published and without a similar condition being
imposed on the subsequent purchaser.

Internal and cover illustrations originally published in John
James Audubon's *Birds of America*, Thomas Bewick's *History of
British Birds, Volumes I & II* and the Knight's Pictorial Museum
of Animated Nature series

Text design by carrdesignstudio.com

A CIP record for this book is available from the British Library

ISBN 978-1-78352-695-6 (hardback)
ISBN 978-1-78352-697-0 (ebook)

Printed in Barcelona by Novoprint

1 3 5 7 9 8 6 4 2

To my mother-in-law, who does not
believe that this is an acceptable way
to make a living

Introduction

HAVE YOU EVER listened to the melodic chirping of birds and wondered what they were trying to communicate?

Some of the world's most brilliant scientists have spent decades studying birdsong to gain an understanding of birds: their society, their needs, their hopes and dreams. Are birds gripped by the paralysing fear that they'll fail to provide for their families? Do they aspire to meaningful careers? Are they frustrated at the pace of social progress in the world?

It turns out that these were the feelings of the scientists and not the birds at all. Advances in machine learning over the past ten years have allowed for detailed scenario analysis of birds and their songs, and multiple computer-driven studies* that compiled years' worth of audio and video recordings came to an astonishing conclusion: most of the time, birds are just saying, 'Fuck off.'

Sometimes they're saying fuck off to predators. Sometimes to other birds. In the studies, scientists found that the birds were

---

* I made these up because this book is fake – but keep that as a secret between you and me and the handful of other nerds who read footnotes.

disproportionately saying fuck off to the scientists studying them, which led to some sober re-examination of their bird-handling protocols.

This astonishing breakthrough has led to re-evaluations of historic recordings, including one analysis that showed US President Lyndon B. Johnson's pet lovebirds telling British Prime Minister Harold Wilson to 'fuck off and keep fucking off until your feet get wet' during a White House visit, and another in which Challenger the bald eagle told Major League Baseball Commissioner Bud Selig to 'find a newer and more interesting way to fuck off' at the 1998 World Series. Most embarrassingly, computer analysis shows that the pigeons in the 'Feed the Birds' scene of Mary Poppins are actually saying, 'Just give us the fucking bread before we die of old age.'

While it would prove impossible to create a definitive listing of every way that birds say fuck off, this book is an attempt to catalogue some of the most common, and to place them into broader societal context, along with identifying bird behaviours and characteristics. And while very few people will have access to the advanced computational power needed to understand birdsong precisely, the hope is that the knowledge contained in this book will allow you to look directly into a bird's eyes and understand it when it tells you to fuck off with that shit.

FUCK OFF WITH THAT SHIT

Part One

LAND BIRDS

Contrary to popular belief, land birds are not flightless birds – they are birds that you don't generally find hanging out on the lake. As such, they have a contrasting set of complaints: where a water bird is likely to advise a holidaymaker on a boogie board to fuck off back to the city, a land bird would more frequently tell a cable repair person to fuck off out of their tree – two completely different sentiments.

FUCK ALL THE WAY OFF

DIRT CHICKEN

Low to the ground and generally silent, the dirt chicken kicks up
a ruckus when stepped on or tripped over.

HABITAT: Underfoot.

IDENTIFYING CHARACTERISTICS: An inability to share blame; repeated
behaviours that lead to the same undesired results.

IF YOU HAVE A POINT, I WOULD LOVE FOR YOU TO FUCKING GET TO IT

PEEVISH RINGNECK

This is a bird that has heard one too many stories and has other shit to get done.

HABITAT: Always on the go between places.

IDENTIFYING CHARACTERISTICS: Rolling eyes and a lot of passive-aggressive sighing noises.

WHY DO YOU THINK I CARE ABOUT THIS?

IS IT THE FUCKING WEEKEND YET?

FOR FUCK'S SAKE

LIGHT-BELLIED DEFEATIST

This bird's frustrated cry is so compelling that the National Society of Pessimists put the light-bellied defeatist on their coat of arms.

HABITAT: Wherever it has nested, it is not good enough.

IDENTIFYING CHARACTERISTICS: Furrowed brow, high blood pressure.

I'M JUST GONNA GET INTO BED AND EAT A WHOLE FUCKING PIE

CAPITULATION FINCH

When the world is too much to handle, the capitulation finch has a nap.

HABITAT: In bed, on the couch, lying on the floor between the bed and the couch.

IDENTIFYING CHARACTERISTICS: Sweatpants.

CONGRATULATIONS ON
SCALING SHIT MOUNTAIN

YOUR
PRIORITIES
ARE FUCKED

FUCK YOU, I'M NOT SORRY

INCOMPUNCTIOUS OWL

This owl's large size and dominating personality allow it to do basically anything it wants.

HABITAT: Wherever it wants to go.

IDENTIFYING CHARACTERISTICS: An alarming lack of empathy.

FUCK YOUR EXCUSES

COME BACK
WHEN YOU
GET YOUR SHIT
TOGETHER

DID YOU EVEN READ THE FUCKING SYLLABUS?

KINGSFIELD'S VULTURE

No animal has ever prevailed in a confrontation with
a kingsfield's vulture.

HABITAT: Educational institutions, usually the kind with gargoyles.

IDENTIFYING CHARACTERISTICS: A steely, emotionless gaze while you
attempt to explain why you're handing in this paper so late.

I AM SUFFERING FROM BULLSHIT FATIGUE

WEARY JACKDAW

A small, vocal bird with an overdeveloped outrage muscle.

HABITAT: Twitter, Facebook, whatever is next.

IDENTIFYING CHARACTERISTICS: Despite being horrified and mentally spent, the weary jackdaw is unable to stop browsing social media.

WHY DID I COME TO WORK TODAY?

FUZZY CHATTERER

You finally got on a roll at the office: you're being productive, you're pleased with your work and you're feeling good about your contribution to the team. Then, like an Eeyore-shaped cloud, the fuzzy chatterer arrives.

HABITAT: Some dark corner of your workplace.

IDENTIFYING CHARACTERISTICS: A sense of imminent doom that the chatterer passes along like the common cold.

YOU ARE THE WORST FUCKING HUMAN

WHO'S IN CHARGE OF THIS FUCKING TRAIN WRECK?

GET THE FUCK
OVER YOURSELF

ONEROUS OSPREY

The most ironic aspect of the onerous osprey is the high regard it holds for itself while denigrating others for the high regard they hold for themselves. Naturally, this irony is lost on them.

HABITAT: Commonly found in the 'eight items or less' line at the supermarket with sixteen items, complaining about the person in front of them with nine items.

IDENTIFYING CHARACTERISTICS: Slightly downy feathers, an unyielding gaze and a completely incomprehensible value system.

I'M NOT STICKING
AROUND TO SEE HOW
THIS SHIT ENDS

THAT'S A LOT OF BULLSHIT FOR A SMALL MAN

HUMPBACKED SPARROW

This incredibly tiny bird makes a lot of noise despite its size.

HABITAT: Hiding behind a username that's a random word and a four-digit number.

IDENTIFYING CHARACTERISTICS: Types in all uppercase, can't read past a headline and is invested in only one thing: 'winning'.

IT APPEARS THAT I OVERESTIMATED THE FUCK OUT OF YOUR INTELLIGENCE

MOTHER WREN

The mother wren gives every one of her hatchlings the benefit of the doubt until it is far too late.

HABITAT: A cozy, suburban home that is simultaneously filled with warm nostalgia and the unrelenting horror of Formica.

IDENTIFYING CHARACTERISTICS: Every conversation with a mother wren eventually turns into a judgmental diatribe on why you can't afford to buy a house.

WHAT IN THE FUCK IS MY LIFE?

HAVE SOME FUCKING DIGNITY

THANKS A LOT, FUCKSTAIN

AGGRO RAVEN

A shiny bird with a pointed beak that delivers cutting evaluations of your personality, manner of dress and ability to function in society.

HABITAT: For whatever reason, there's always one in your circle of friends.

IDENTIFYING CHARACTERISTICS: A pyromaniacal zest for burning bridges.

GET SOME FUCKING POPCORN, IT'S SHITSHOW TIME

COLLARED OBSERVER PENGUIN

Thriving on the conflict of other birds, the collared observer penguin spends its time watching – and occasionally instigating – fights that it refuses to participate in.

HABITAT: Always the sidelines, never the fray.

IDENTIFYING CHARACTERISTICS: A black hole of emptiness where others would have values.

I AM A
GODDAMNED
DELIGHT

TALKING TO
YOU IS FUCKING
EXHAUSTING

TODAY IS INTERNATIONAL STOP BEING A FUCKFACE DAY

CANTANKEROUS REDWING

This bird is strongly attracted to irritants like noise, modern fashion trends and the expression of joy.

HABITAT: You cannot avoid the cantankerous redwing, especially at parties.

IDENTIFYING CHARACTERISTICS: A militaristic lack of fun.

WHO PUT THESE DUMBFUCKS IN CHARGE?

DISAVOWAL PHEASANT

This pheasant resides in a world where it has no responsibility for the state of things.

HABITAT: Previously found in the endless headers of a forwarded email chain, but has more recently been spotted on Facebook.

IDENTIFYING CHARACTERISTICS: Highly amplified outrage, and a willingness to believe memes.

YOU'RE A FUCKING DISGRACE TO NEPOTISM

TINY HORNBEAK

The tiny hornbeak will never get a promotion while the boss still has unemployed nephews.

HABITAT: Often found sulking in a cubicle near the back where the fluorescent tubes are flickering.

IDENTIFYING CHARACTERISTICS: The large ears and weak chin of one whose parents believed in keeping things in the family.

OWN YOUR BULLSHIT

THAT'S A MASSIVE FUCKING OVERREACTION

THIS SHIT MAKES ME TIRED

FUCK OFF,
I'M READING

OH YEAH, FUCK ALL OF THAT SHIT

PINK JOINER

The pink joiner is somewhat poorly named, as it is not a joiner. It is also not pink.

HABITAT: Wherever activities are announced, pink joiners will be there to belittle them.

IDENTIFYING CHARACTERISTICS: An air of above-it-all aloofness used to disguise the fact that it is basically not good at anything.

LET ME GUESS: YOU'RE A FUCKING DIMWIT

SPECKLED ARBITER

The arbiter family of birds prefer to perch very high in trees, where they are ideally placed to look down on everyone.

HABITAT: Often found on horses – the taller the better.

IDENTIFYING CHARACTERISTICS: The speckled arbiter is most easily recognised by its belief that it alone is qualified to judge what should be considered *Star Trek*.

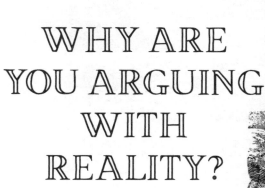

WHY ARE YOU ARGUING WITH REALITY?

UNEQUIVOCAL EAGLE

This eagle perceives the world in high-contrast monochrome and is only able to identify simple shapes.

HABITAT: Reddit.

IDENTIFYING CHARACTERISTICS: Absurdly literal, unable to recognise rhetorical questions, and willing to believe any information presented in a graph or pie chart.

I NEED A FUCKING NAP

FUCK-A-DOODLE-DOO

I DIDN'T UNDERSTAND YOUR ARGUMENT BECAUSE IT'S BULLSHIT

MOTHERRRRR FUCKERRRRR

ARTICULATE CROW

This bird is loud as fuck.

FUCK OFF

WRATHFUL SPARROW

This tiny bird has a narrow emotional range, from irate to choleric. Keep your distance unless you want to get pecked.

HABITAT: Generally makes its home in a place that will surely cause it to lose its shit, like the comment section of an online newspaper.

IDENTIFYING CHARACTERISTICS: Marked by a strong red colouration and steam blowing out of its ears.

I AM FUCKING MAGNIFICENT

VAINGLORIOUS GREBE

When you lock eyes with a vainglorious grebe, you find yourself filled with doubts and concerns. Are you underdressed? Will it demand to see your invitation? Do you really belong here?

HABITAT: Found only in the most elegant of forests, the vainglorious grebe prefers to nest in imported designer fabrics.

IDENTIFYING CHARACTERISTICS: Brilliant colours, massive sunglasses.

HOW ABOUT I JUST DO YOUR FUCKING JOB FOR YOU?

VOCATIONAL TERN

The vocational tern isn't here to make things better; the vocational tern is here to entertain itself.

HABITAT: Most frequently found at the part of the meeting where everything goes to shit.

IDENTIFYING CHARACTERISTICS: Smaller vocational terns are passive-aggressive, whereas larger ones are simply aggressive. Though sometimes it can be hard to tell the two apart.

BY GOD, YOU'RE A DUMB MOTHERFUCKER

FLABBERGAST'S FINCH

The flabbergast's finch expects the best of everyone,
even when there is no evidence that it should expect anything
other than the worst.

HABITAT: Generally found in the orbit of people who will
only disappoint.

IDENTIFYING CHARACTERISTICS: An unusual capacity for surprise.

I WOULD PAY REAL MONEY FOR YOU TO FUCK OFF

FRACTIOUS QUAIL

If you find yourself having angered a fractious quail, the best advice would be to run for as long as you can in any direction without looking back.

HABITAT: Keep running! Don't look back!

IDENTIFYING CHARACTERISTICS: A very sharp beak – Christ, that hurts. Why did you stop running?

LOOK AT THIS GODDAMN TURD FARM

I NEED COFFEE

HOW LONG UNTIL THE FUCKING APOCALYPSE?

FATALISTIC FALCON

Like a giant rain cloud or a swarm of killer beers, the fatalistic
falcon darkens the horizon as it approaches.

HABITAT: It doesn't matter, we're all doomed.

IDENTIFYING CHARACTERISTICS: Aware that the end is near, the fatalistic
falcon can be heard sighing heavily and dragging its feet.

DO
NOT
TRY

FUCK
WEEKDAYS

YES, I WANT TO HEAR ALL ABOUT YOUR BULLSHIT

GREY-WINGED ENABLER

It is unclear what the motives of the grey-winged enabler are, but its impact is easy to assess: it draws out the worst instincts in everyone it encounters.

HABITAT: At the bar, encouraging just one more drink.

IDENTIFYING CHARACTERISTICS: It is somehow immune to any negative impacts of its behaviour.

THIS SHIT IS TOO MUCH EVEN FOR ME

ABDICATING SPARROW

When the going gets tough, this hardy little bird fucks off out of self-preservation.

HABITAT: Prefers to nest in low-bullshit areas.

IDENTIFYING CHARACTERISTICS: Hard to tell what it looks like from the front.

I'M A BIG DEAL ON THE FUCKING INTERNET

BEGUILED SWIFT

The beguiled swift's casual Instagram self-portrait has been art-directed by a professional and retouched to within an inch of its life: clearly this bird is an Influencer.

HABITAT: When it isn't buried beak-first in its smartphone, the beguiled swift is tapping away at its computer.

IDENTIFYING CHARACTERISTICS: Frequent talk of metrics, engagement, CPM, ratio, Alexa rank, Klout score and other things that are clearly not real.

I LIKE YOU
BETTER WHEN
YOU SHUT THE
FUCK UP

IF I WANTED ADVICE
FROM AN ASSHOLE, I
WOULD HAVE ASKED
ON THE INTERNET

YOU ARE CORDIALLY INVITED
TO SNIFF MY BUTTHOLE

INDECOROUS GULL

The indecorous gull has abandoned all attempts to participate in polite society, but can't quite understand why its party invitations have dried up.

HABITAT: It tries to nest where all the other birds are but is constantly rebuffed. It naturally sees this as a failing of the other birds.

IDENTIFYING CHARACTERISTICS: If you ask the indecorous gull, the problem is definitely society and not the thing where it is always being an asshole.

LOOK, ASSHOLE, I DON'T HAVE TIME TO EXPLAIN

BASICALLY, YOU'RE FUCKING INCOMPETENT

ASTUTE OWLS

As much as you don't want an astute owl to be correct, the astute owl is correct.

HABITAT: Lurking nearby whenever you make a mistake.

IDENTIFYING CHARACTERISTICS: An unnerving sense of timing.

STUFF THAT IN YOUR GARBAGE HOLE

LONG-LEGGED PANACEA

The long-legged panacea has no time for your poorly researched opinion.

HABITAT: Let's be honest: you're only at the receiving end of this bird's wrath because you tweeted a garbage reply at it.

IDENTIFYING CHARACTERISTICS: Extreme height that lends extra authoritative weight to all of its pronouncements.

HOW HAVE
YOU SURVIVED SO
MANY YEARS
OF BEING
AN IMBECILE?

THAT
WAS THE
STUPIDEST

LEAVE THIS TO THE FUCKING PROFESSIONALS

FALLACY'S BLACKBIRD

Whenever conversations requiring expertise and nuance occur, fallacy's blackbird is there to muddy the waters.

HABITAT: Academia, panel shows, letters to the editor.

IDENTIFYING CHARACTERISTICS: Hubris, misplaced confidence and a history of embarrassing deleted tweets.

WHEN DID I GET SO FUCKING OLD?

CONVERSANT OWL

One day, the conversant owl woke up and realised that it was focused on the wrong parts of life.

HABITAT: On eBay, trying to buy back its childhood.

IDENTIFYING CHARACTERISTICS: Profound sadness for the passing of an era that probably never existed.

FUCK IT, I'M NOT COOKING DINNER

ENERVATED EAGLE

This family of birds (and their soul-crushing day jobs) keep chain restaurants in business.

HABITAT: A cubicle, being drained of their vitality for too many hours of the day, and then going home to do laundry.

IDENTIFYING CHARACTERISTICS: Unread books, abandoned hobbies and a Netflix queue that only grows.

NO FUCKING WAY

WHAT THE FUCK
IS HAPPENING
RIGHT NOW?

OF COURSE YOU DIDN'T PLAN FOR THIS FUCKING CATASTROPHE

FORETHOUGHT'S HERON

When things have gone horribly wrong, you hear the distant call of the forethought's heron: 'I tollllld you sooooooo.'

HABITAT: Never to be found in the location where you are planning; always to be found in the location where you are doing the post-mortem.

IDENTIFYING CHARACTERISTICS: Grey feathers, long beak, the belief that all events are predictable.

Look at these fucking idiots

CONSUMMATE FALCON

The consummate falcon's distinctive cry is a declaration that it does not even own a television, and that only sheep would watch something as unchallenging and low-brow as *The Bachelor*.

HABITAT: Can usually be found watching *The Bachelor* and then tweeting angrily about it afterwards. From a pseudonymous account, naturally.

IDENTIFYING CHARACTERISTICS: An encyclopedic knowledge of all previous contestants on The Bachelor and what they're up to right now.

NOT TODAY

SPOTTED DO-NOTHING

The spotted do-nothing is aghast at the state of the modern world
and wishes we could all just go back to the way things were when
it was young.

HABITAT: Often found moaning in the comments under political
articles, though they also appear with regularity wherever
millennials are mentioned.

IDENTIFYING CHARACTERISTICS: No conception of their part in making
the world worse, and no suggestions for how to make it better.

THAT'S

SNITCHES
GET STITCHES

Make

it end

Here comes bullshit

FORECAST CARDINAL

This bird has the fortunate ability to see what's coming, but an unfortunate lack of ambition to do anything about it.

HABITAT: Cable news panel shows, dark web internet forums and Thanksgiving dinner with the extended family.

IDENTIFYING CHARACTERISTICS: Their bookshelves are lined with dystopian fiction, but they can't be bothered to get the tinfoil from the kitchen to line their hat.

Look at this clusterfuck

I have feelings

Fuck emotions

Keep it in your pants

APPRAISING BLUEBIRD

If you don't want the appraising bluebird's opinion on something, you should not show that something to the appraising bluebird.

HABITAT: For some incomprehensible reason, people constantly seek out the appraising bluebird. It doesn't hide, but it sure as hell doesn't have a neon sign by its nest that says, 'I WANT TO HEAR YOUR HOT TAKES.'

IDENTIFYING CHARACTERISTICS: While its victims wish it were not the case, the appraising bluebird feels no obligation to be kind when replying to an unsolicted opinion.

Fuck off

DEPARTURE MARTIN

Departure martins will tell you when it is time to go, where you should go and what you should do once you get there.

HABITAT: It is not generally welcome in one's living room, but on the other hand it will garner applause when it has told off a particularly obnoxious patron in the line at Starbucks.

IDENTIFYING CHARACTERISTICS: Good sense, strong moral fibre and a complete inability to leave shit alone.

Shut the fuck up

BULL
SHIT

LISTEN TO MY OPINIONS

TUMULTUOUS TERN

Like some kind of verbal fire hose, the tumultuous tern spews out an endless stream of poorly researched invective.

HABITAT: The official bird of Twitter.

IDENTIFYING CHARACTERISTICS: Compact, loud, unable to process or synthesise feedback and counterarguments, and, most importantly, it is blue.

HOLY SHIT

I NEED
CAFFEINE

VIRTUOUS VULTURE

This vulture moves at a glacial pace that makes one wonder if it is still alive, but then it suddenly snaps into action at the first sign that someone, somewhere, has made a mistake. Correcting a hapless idiot is the virtuous vulture's raison d'être, and in the same way that a hammer treats all problems as nails, the virtuous vulture views all other living creatures as hapless idiots.

HABITAT: Wherever you find them, you don't want to be there anymore.

IDENTIFYING CHARACTERISTICS: When a virtuous vulture approaches, a kind of static energy crackles in the air. If you can learn to identify this sensation, you can get the fuck out of there while there's still time.

WE ALL
SAW YOU
FUCK
THAT UP

I'm already drunk

WHEN WILL IT ALL FUCKING END?

YOU HAVE A HIGH OPINION OF YOURSELF FOR A GIGANTIC FUCKING DUNCE

I SEE WE'RE BACK TO EATING OUR OWN POOP

I'M NOT LAUGHING, FUCKWEED

YOU DIM MOTHERFUCKER, SCIENCE IS REAL

COMPETENT OWL

Competent owls hold the mistaken belief that being right allows one to be a dickhead.

HABITAT: Causing more harm than good in arguments with complete strangers.

IDENTIFYING CHARACTERISTICS: Righteous anger that the massive blind spot around their own behaviour causes others to ignore their message.

THE WORLD IS A SHITBARGE

HIPSTER PELICAN

'There's a real magic to vintage vinyl,' the hipster pelican tells you. 'Decades of experiences and emotions have been absorbed right into the LP; you can't get that from a streaming service.'

HABITAT: Probably at the vegan, locally sourced juice bar.

IDENTIFYING CHARACTERISTICS: Carefully coiffed plumage – plenty above and below the face, but absolutely none on the sides – and carefully selected items in its nest, all curated to tell you a story about how much this bird cares.

HONESTLY, I CAN'T TAKE ANY MORE OF THIS SHIT

JUST FUCKING GOOGLE IT

YOU ASSBAG

VITUPERATIVE LARK

This is one of those birds that you don't see until it is too late.

HABITAT: You wish you knew, just so you could avoid it.

IDENTIFYING CHARACTERISTICS: Swooping down from a great height, it lets out an ear-splitting screech right before it rips off your wig and carries it back to its nest.

THE CORRECT ANSWER
IS FUCK OFF

I HAVE NEVER MET
A PROUDER IDIOT

SAY THAT SHIT TO MY FACE

COMBED GOSHAWK

The problem with insulting a combed goshawk is that it will find out about it and confront you in the most uncomfortable way possible.

HABITAT: Always where other people are around, because it isn't really humiliation if it happens in private.

IDENTIFYING CHARACTERISTICS: Loud voice, unyielding glare, endless patience.

TAKE SOME RESPONSIBILITY FOR YOUR BULLSHIT

INCULPATE CHICKEN

Like the proverbial sparrow with a machine gun, the inculpate chicken is small but dangerous.

HABITAT: Wherever there is blame to be laid.

IDENTIFYING CHARACTERISTICS: Most easily found by following the trail of bewildered dudes lying on the ground, trying to process being held accountable for something for the first time in their lives.

GET
FUUUUCKED

I AM FULLY
AWARE OF HOW
FUCKING AWESOME
I AM

THIS IS A BIG FRIGGING
WASTE OF ENERGY

OBVIATED WARBLER

While some would call its lifestyle choice 'sloth', the obviated warbler prefers to call it 'a differentiated set of priorities'.

HABITAT: Anywhere, as long as there is Netflix.

IDENTIFYING CHARACTERISTICS: A distinctive, keening song that it sings from sunrise to sunset while staying in the same position.

WHERE IS YOUR FUCKING BRAIN?

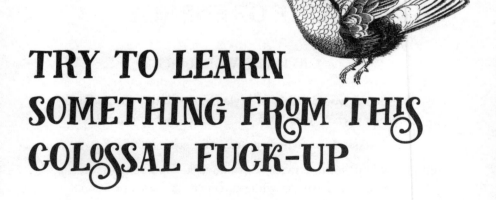

TRY TO LEARN SOMETHING FROM THIS COLOSSAL FUCK-UP

THIS IS SOME GRADE-SCHOOL BULLSHIT

MATURE BUZZARD

The mature buzzard is here to remind you of what you should and should not be doing, based on the elapsed time since your birth.

HABITAT: Generally found where there is fun to be had, discouraging it.

IDENTIFYING CHARACTERISTICS: It wears a button-down shirt with a tie; don't listen to anything it has to say.

EAT FARTS

IS THIS NEW BULLSHIT OR JUST THE SAME OLD BULLSHIT?

ABSTRUSE HERON

This small, irritating bird asks questions that it already knows the answer to.

HABITAT: The back of your mind.

IDENTIFYING CHARACTERISTICS: Persistence, nagging, sudden appearances when things are going well.

CAN THIS
SHIT BE
SOMEONE
ELSE'S
PROBLEM?

YOU ARE NOT
CAPABLE OF
PRODUCING A
USEFUL RESULT

OBJECTIVELY SPEAKING, THIS IS BULLSHIT

I LIVE IN A FUCKING TREE, IDIOT

GO AWAY, DICKBAG

DOMINION TEAL

The dominion teal is notably territorial but determines its territory on a whim.

HABITAT: Today it might be this patch of grass by the edge of the pond, and tomorrow it might be the fourth barstool from the left. But no matter where it decides is its territory, you are the interloper, even if you've been sitting on the stool for the last hour.

IDENTIFYING CHARACTERISTICS: Avoid making direct eye contact with a dominion teal.

FUCK THIS SHIT,
I'M OUT OF HERE

I HAVE PUT UP
WITH ENOUGH BULLSHIT
FOR THREE LIFETIMES

THIS IS SOME BAROQUE DOGSHIT

DISCERNING BUFFLEHEAD

While the discerning bufflehead isn't going to put up with your shit, it does appreciate the amount of effort that went into it. The bufflehead merely wishes you had put that effort into your job instead.

HABITAT: Sitting directly across from you during your annual review.

IDENTIFYING CHARACTERISTICS: A lot of sighing.

YOU SELF-IMPORTANT PIECE OF SHIT

SANDWICH TERN

While most bird enthusiasts assume that the sandwich tern was named for the food item that it frequently steals from picnickers, it was actually named for the Earl of Sandwich, a self-important piece of shit.

WHY AM I SO FUCKING UNLOVABLE?

GET OFF MY LAWN

THAT'S A BIG FUCKING NOPE

JUST FUCKING GREAT

SARDONIC JAY

With a longer lifespan than most birds, the sardonic jay tends to become jaded as it ages. At some point, everyone assumes that any expression of happiness or enthusiasm from the sardonic jay must be sarcasm, and after a while even the jay itself is unsure. Maybe it was never happy at all.

HABITAT: A home that was expensive – that should be a sign it's a good house, right? This is a nice place to live, right? God, why did I spend all this money on this house?

IDENTIFYING CHARACTERISTICS: A quiver at the edge of its smile.

I CAN'T DEAL WITH YOUR SHIT TODAY

THAT'S NOT HOW REALITY WORKS, DUMBSHIT

NOW WOULD
BE A GREAT
TIME FOR
YOU TO SHUT
YOUR FUCKING
MOUTH

ARE YOU
FUCKING
SERIOUS?

TIME FOR A VACATION FROM YOUR BULLSHIT

FALTER OWL

The falter owl is driven by an astute sense of self-preservation. When it finds itself surrounded by other owls that are mentally or physically draining, it will frequently disappear for an hour.

HABITAT: If you haven't seen it for a while, sometimes you can find it in the bathroom.

IDENTIFYING CHARACTERISTICS: Sometimes it says it forgot to get something from the shop; sometimes it remembers that it left the oven on; and sometimes it just has to take this important call even though no one heard its phone buzz.

YOU ARE AN IRRESPONSIBLE CRAP PILE

PRECIPITOUS EAGLE

Charming, fun to be around, generous with its time and energy – everyone loves the precipitous eagle, at least at first.

HABITAT: It probably still lives in the basement of its parents' house.

IDENTIFYING CHARACTERISTICS: It can be hard to tell a precipitous eagle from a run-of-the-mill eagle until you've been around it for a while – the pattern of late arrivals, broken promises and unfinished projects takes time to recognise. But once you do recognise it, you can bake it into your plans and avoid a lot of messy family drama.

WELL, AREN'T YOU HOT SHIT

I DIDN'T GET OUT OF BED TO DEAL WITH THIS BULLSHIT

BETTER LUCK NEXT TIME, FUCKNUTS

OVERBEARING HERON

This heron's primary source of joy is the misfortune of others. And while it always feels like their comeuppance is just around the corner, it never seems to arrive.

HABITAT: You'll be having a perfectly ordinary conversation, and the overbearing heron will swoop in: 'Did you hear about Sharon?' it asks in a way that you know means it is about to tell you about Sharon.

IDENTIFYING CHARACTERISTICS: Through some alchemical combination of tone of voice and body language, this bird is able to convey 'this is a secret' in a voice loud enough for everyone to hear.

I AM SO THANKFUL
THAT YOU ARE HERE TO
EXPLAIN MY JOB TO ME

APPRENTICE EIDER

The apprentice eider is a formidable predator from an early age.

HABITAT: If it isn't at its desk, check by the water cooler.

IDENTIFYING CHARACTERISTICS: A thousand-yard stare that cuts into your soul, a snarky attitude and the ability to turn any offer of assistance into an insult.

FUCK YOU,
I'M HILARIOUS

I AM SO FUCKING HIGH

AREN'T YOU A FANCY MOTHERFUCKER

REGARD'S FLAMINGO

Stemming from a deep lack of self-esteem, the regard's flamingo nitpicks any outward display of success by other birds. At first this seems reasonable – you ask yourself, 'Am I being ostentatious?' You stop wearing your nice watch to work. But listen, you worked hard for that watch. Does it bring you some small amount of joy during the day? Then wear the goddamn watch.

HABITAT: Always in the orbit of successful people.

IDENTIFYING CHARACTERISTICS: Great-looking shoes that they will stress to you they got in the sale.

GOOD LUCK WITH YOUR BULLSHIT

FUCK ALL OF THAT

CALM
YOUR SHIT
DOWN AND
TRY AGAIN

FEMINISM IS FOR EVERYONE, DIPSHIT

FUCK WORK

Listen, none of us wants to be here today. You muttering about it isn't helping. Let's all get shit done until 3 p.m. and then have a 'team meeting' where we just do Twitter on our phones for a couple of hours and then we can get the fuck out of here without losing our health insurance.

IT'S TOO EARLY IN THE MORNING FOR ME TO TRY

AMBITIOUS SHRIKE

There is always something impeding the ambitious shrike. It could be a hair appointment, or a recall on its car, or a general distrust of Wednesdays in the middle of the month. Whatever it is, overcoming it is virtually impossible.

HABITAT: At the bottom of the stack ranking, wondering how it scored so low.

IDENTIFYING CHARACTERISTICS: A truly astounding ability to describe things in a way that puts all blame and responsibility onto the nebulous energies of the universe.

CAN YOU GO
BE A FUCKING
GARBAGE PERSON
SOMEWHERE ELSE,
PLEASE?

YOU ARE A
SPECTACULAR
AMOUNT OF
WRONG

WELCOME TO MUTESVILLE, FUCKO

OBLIVIOUS PHEASANT

The whole point of muting someone on social media is so that
you don't hear from them anymore, but they have no idea
and keep hooting into the void. When you announce it, they
know you're not listening and turn their unwanted attention to
another victim. Please, for the rest of our sakes, don't tell them
that you're muting them.

YOU CAN GO EAT A DICK AS FAR AS I'M CONCERNED

I'M GLAD I'M NOT THE ONLY ONE DEALING WITH THIS SHIT

WELL, THAT WAS A FUCKING WASTE OF RESOURCES

HUSBAND OWL

No one is more fiercely protective of corporate assets than the husband owl. The Post-it note rationing system, the binder re-use policy and the company-wide maximum on the number of colours in a printed document were all the brilliant efforts of the husband owl.

HABITAT: In the stockroom, wondering why they cannot find love.

IDENTIFYING CHARACTERISTICS: A photographic memory, but only for the pettiest of things.

HOLD
ON TO
YOUR
SHIT

GODDAMN FUCKING SHIT

I'VE PASSED
BETTER IDEAS
OUT OF MY
BUTTHOLE

THE FUCK YOU SAY?

UGH

UNIDENTIFIED SPECIMEN

While little is known about this as-yet unidentified bird, it is clear
that its bones were picked clean by life.

FRANKLY, I EXPECTED MORE

Part Two

WATER BIRDS

Found in ponds, lakes and rivers, water birds frequently have words for cottagers and outdoorsmen – and those words are, 'Take your £600 hiking boots and your fucking survival pants from the internet back to the city, chump.'

EVERYBODY FUCK OFF
FOR A WHILE

HERMIT SANDPIPER

The best way to connect with a hermit sandpiper is by text
message, even if it lives next door.

HABITAT: While it tends to nest in accessible areas, it actively avoids
contact with humans.

IDENTIFYING CHARACTERISTICS: You'd have to find one in the first place.

HERE IS THE VALIDATION
YOU CRAVE

BULLSEYE GULL

The bullseye gull's detailed understanding of what makes a person tick allows it to deliver laser-guided criticism directly into the heart of its prey. Do not tell it about your childhood, your insecurities, your hobbies, your career – hell, just walk in the other direction if you see one coming.

HABITAT: Once you've encountered a bullseye gull, it lives in your head forever.

IDENTIFYING CHARACTERISTICS: Eyes that see into your soul; razor-sharp claws (at least, metaphorically).

I CALLED YOUR MOTHER TO COME PICK YOU UP

WHITE-BELLIED COSSET

The white-bellied cosset takes charge of younger birds in its orbit, teaching them about etiquette, how to save money for a house, workplace norms and more, regardless of the desires of the younger birds.

HABITAT: A cubicle full of Beanie Babies and cut-out magazine pictures.

IDENTIFYING CHARACTERISTICS: If you cross a white-bellied cosset, expect that it will call your parents and express disappointment in you.

YOU ARE VERY BRAVE TO MAKE SUCH A GIGANTIC ASS OF YOURSELF

RED-WINGED DEHORT

Where other birds offer encouraging words, the red-winged dehort focuses on the worst-case scenario.

HABITAT: Karaoke bars, open mics, presentations, the dance floor.

IDENTIFYING CHARACTERISTICS: You can tell the red-winged dehort is near because it emits an unpleasant, damp sensation that blankets the area.

DO YOU THINK I'M A FUCKING IDIOT?

HAUGHTY PENGUIN

'He who smelt it dealt it' is a childish expression with limited application to adult life, though it does neatly characterise the protestations of the haughty penguin.

HABITAT: Wherever the fucking idiots hang out these days.

IDENTIFYING CHARACTERISTICS: Keen sense of smell, peculiar speckle pattern on its belly and an inability to distinguish when it is, in fact, being a fucking idiot.

WAS BEING A DIPSHIT A JOB REQUIREMENT?

THANKS FOR NOTHING, FUCKFACE

WHY DID YOU WAIT UNTIL
THE LAST FUCKING MINUTE?

YOUR INPUT IS NOT REQUIRED

DON'T MAKE ME FUCK UP
ALL YOUR SHIT

GO FUCK A TREE

HAVE SOME FUCKING WINE

PRETEND I'M STILL LISTENING

I DO NOT WANT TO HEAR YOUR FUCKING LIFE STORY

SMOOTH-BELLIED EXASPERATOR

The motionless, dead eyes of the smooth-bellied exasperator are at odds with its never-silent mouth.

HABITAT: Found at parties, asking open-ended questions out of a sense of duty.

IDENTIFYING CHARACTERISTICS: A total lack of interest in you, your employment, your hobbies or your family.

PRETTY SURE YOU
MADE THAT SHIT UP

MAYBE TOMORROW YOU'LL BE LESS OF A SHITHEAD

FUCK THE OUTDOORS

BUFF PETREL

The buff petrel is oblivious to the visual and auditory cues that you do not wish to go on a hike with it. 'It will be fun,' it keeps saying. You know that this is not true.

HABITAT: If it's not halfway up the side of a mountain or deep in an old-growth forest, you can find it in the sporting goods store, buying more carabiners.

IDENTIFYING CHARACTERISTICS: Clad in moisture-wicking, high-tech fabrics and sporting multiple exercise trackers.

Nobody asked you

What is this shit?

MENDACIOUS RAVEN

The mendacious raven knows exactly what this shit is; its cawing is just an attempt to get you to interact with it. And don't get me wrong, it can be fun for a while. Just stop before you also become a mendacious raven.

HABITAT: There's one in every office.

IDENTIFYING CHARACTERISTICS: If it bites you, you'll turn into a complaining, feathered mess when the moon is full or when prime-time network TV is on.

Fuck
this

Bleh

This place is bullshit

MOANING VIREO

If it isn't the venue, it's the DJ. If it isn't the DJ, it's the clientele. Or the lighting. Or the decor. Or the quality of the alcohol served at the bar. Or the softness of the towels in the toilet. Or any other excuse to not have a good time.

HABITAT: In your social circle, though you're wondering why you continue to invite it out with you.

IDENTIFYING CHARACTERISTICS: Like a whirling vortex that consumes fun and enjoyment.

Go to the fucking library

LITERATE PLOVER

Let's be real: there's no way you found this book at the
library. Still, libraries are fucking awesome, you should go
to them and get some books that aren't just a bunch of
pictures of birds and swear words.

We both know
that's bullshit

Blah blah blah

This is my surprised face

CRUSHED TURACO

The turaco has sprained its indignation muscle, and all it has left is a sad kind of resignation. It isn't quite nihilism, but it involves a lot of Netflix and booze.

HABITAT: This bed is comfortable… Why would it get out of this comfortable bed?

IDENTIFYING CHARACTERISTICS: A collection of blankets and pillows, sometimes arranged into a fort.

Fuck no

OSTENTATIOUS OSPREY

This bird is in a constant state of discomfort for the sake of fashion.

HABITAT: You can find it trying not to trip over its own feet on the short walk between its luxury car and the mall.

IDENTIFYING CHARACTERISTICS: Absurdly gigantic sunglasses, a watch the size of a tin of tuna and shoes too impractical to wear for any length of time.

I'm fancy

Your idea can fuck off

Fight me

TRUCULENT HAWK

It wasn't you, don't worry about it. The hawk just wants to have an argument. It lives a small, lonely life and thinks that it will feel better if it is able to hurt someone else, verbally or physically, to show that it isn't at the bottom of the food chain. You can walk away with your head held high, knowing that is exactly where it is and where it deserves to be.

HABITAT: Bars, clubs, Twitter.

IDENTIFYING CHARACTERISTICS: If you look into its eyes for long enough, that defiance melts into depression.

I'm done with your shit

Tastes like bullshit

TURN AROUND AND FUCK RIGHT OFF

GIMME A FUCKIN' BREAK

FUCK THIS SHITAPALOOZA

DEPRECATING GOOSE

Experienced birders know to avoid the deprecating goose – it's territorial and aggressive, and its bite leaves a mark for weeks.

HABITAT: No matter where you put your tent, you've just put it beside a nest of deprecating geese. Get out the topical antiseptic – you're gonna need it.

IDENTIFYING CHARACTERISTICS: Did it bite you? Yes, you spotted one. You're lucky to still have all of your fingers.

GET
YOUR SHIT
TOGETHER

LOOK AT THIS
GODDAMN
SHITSHOW

WHERE'S THE FUCKING GIN?

ENLIGHTENED GOOSANDER

This flexible, mellow water bird takes the entire world with a pinch of salt around the top of a shot glass.

HABITAT: Found in almost every climate, making friends with the bartender.

IDENTIFYING CHARACTERISTICS: You could argue that more of the buttons on its shirt could be done up, but somehow it's making it work.

WHAT THE FUCK IS WRONG WITH PEOPLE?

PLEASE TELL ME MORE ABOUT MY OWN GODDAMN EXPERIENCES

I AM GOING TO FUCK OFF NOW

RECOGNISANT DUCK

The recognisant duck is keenly attuned to the emotional make-up of a room, and therefore knows exactly when it's time to take off.

HABITAT: It left the party a vital fifteen minutes before you did.

IDENTIFYING CHARACTERISTICS: It leaves a trail of quizzical 'She was just here!' exclamations in its wake.

I HAVE NO FURTHER INTEREST
IN YOUR BULLSHIT

CAN YOU FUCK OFF AND NEVER
UN-FUCK OFF?

EAT WOODCHIPS, FUCKSTICK

GET BENT

YOU ARE FUCKING RIDICULOUS

SMEW

The smew is possibly the most disagreeable family of birds. The expression 'do not fuck with a smew' is folk wisdom rooted in fact.

HABITAT: Often found in executive suites, penthouse apartments or Parliament.

IDENTIFYING CHARACTERISTICS: While they come in many sizes, shapes and colours, smews are all aggressive, territorial and strangely attuned to your insecurities.

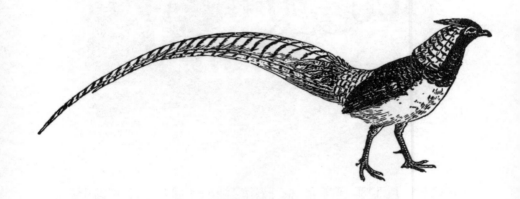

CAN YOUR BULLSHIT WAIT
UNTIL TOMORROW?

DECAMPING GULL

It's 4.52 p.m. Why are you bringing me this now?

I'M SURE THAT SOUNDED GREAT IN YOUR HEAD

REMIND ME: ARE YOU A FUCKING IMBECILE?

PALPABLE RANGER

A vital part of our ecosystem, the palpable ranger provides an important public service: asking the questions that we all know the answer to.

HABITAT: Can be found in guest columns, talking-head TV spots or, most stressfully, conducting your job interview.

IDENTIFYING CHARACTERISTICS: It always seems to be much more prepared than you are.

DO NOT CARE, GOODBYE

IT MUST BE DICKHEAD SEASON

BALLS

ROYAL SWIFT

Known for its majesty and grace, the royal swift makes only a single sound: a breathy, frustrated release.

HABITAT: Facing the television, watching the news.

IDENTIFYING CHARACTERISTICS: The royal swift will freeze in place, eyes locked on the screen, unable to move or change the channel. Shimmering lines of heat radiate from its head. A pulsing vein, usually on the temple or neck, appears dangerously close to rupturing. But the royal swift will keep watching right up until its head explodes.

ME SAYING I
LIKE SOMETHING
IS NOT AN
INVITATION
TO A FUCKING
DEBATE

I DIDN'T LISTEN TO YOUR VOICEMAIL
BECAUSE WE LIVE IN THE GODDAMN
TWENTY-FIRST CENTURY

MAYBE TRY NOT BEING
A DICKHEAD

COUNSELLOR SWALLOW

The counsellor swallow offers up what should be obvious advice but that, nevertheless, people still need.

HABITAT: Once they lived in newsprint columns, but these days they are more commonly found on blogs.

IDENTIFYING CHARACTERISTICS: A surprised or perplexed expression: 'Isn't this just common sense?'

YOU'VE CORNERED THE
MARKET ON STUPID SHIT

THIS IS A FUCKING GARBAGE FIRE

WELL, AREN'T YOU JUST THE KING OF SHIT MOUNTAIN

ESTIMATE'S WIGEON

Your accomplishments, aspirations and accolades mean nothing to an estimate's wigeon. The more you talk about yourself, the less it likes you.

HABITAT: Sometimes it contributes unsolicited reviews of your work on Twitter that you are able to talk your publisher into using on the back cover of your book.

IDENTIFYING CHARACTERISTICS: Impeccable credentials; no sense of humour.

N 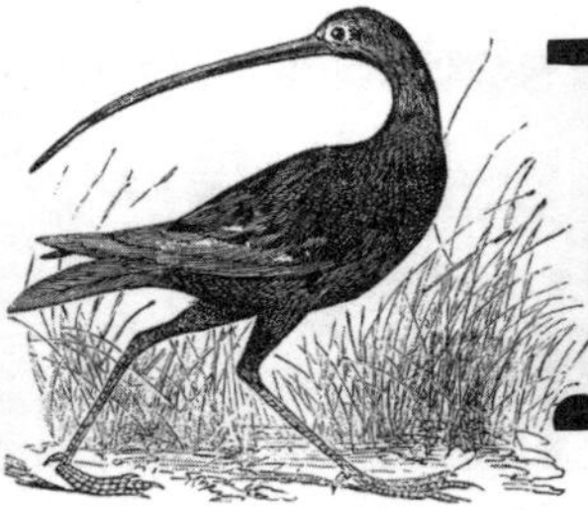 PE

YOU ARE BY FAR THE STUPIDEST FUCKER
I HAVE EVER MET

I AM IGNORING YOUR SHIT

WHY ARE YOU STILL TALKING?

SNUB GULL

Life has piled bullshit up in front of the snub gull, from its terrible
name to its habitat in the swamp. And while the snub gull is
generally patient, at some point everything becomes too much.
If you're lucky, it will just walk away from you. If you're unlucky,
you'll lose a finger first.

HABITAT: The shitty bottom end of shit marsh, at the base of shit hill,
shaded by shit trees. But at least it has a partial view of shit lake.

IDENTIFYING CHARACTERISTICS: It appears to not be registering
any of the shit around it, giving no visible reaction to the
growing shitpile. Then all of a sudden, it'll shiver. If you see
the shiver, it's too late for you.

OH, HONEY, NO

DIAL THAT SHIT WAY BACK

FUCK THIS,
I'M GOING
BACK TO
BED

I DO NOT NEED YOUR SHIT

WHADDUP, WIENERS?

SHINDIG'S MALLARD

Because it is inappropriately jocular and abusive in an upbeat way, it can be confusing to encounter a shindig's mallard. Were you just insulted? Should you be upset? Why are you laughing?

HABITAT: Near the water cooler or some other vital area of the workplace that you can't completely avoid.

IDENTIFYING CHARACTERISTICS: A wide, toothy grin and the smell of cheap aftershave.

TOODLE-OO, FUCKFACE

IS IT DUMBFUCK O'CLOCK
ALREADY?

WHAT ARE YOU, THE FUCKING GENITALS POLICE?

BAILIWICK GULL

The bailiwick gulls may have moved their meetings out of dimly lit church basements and into Facebook groups, but their sense of morality has remained firmly in the 1950s.

HABITAT: Cable news shows, opinion columns and other places where impotent rage is found.

IDENTIFYING CHARACTERISTICS: An obsession with the way that other people live and the need to exert some form of control that it clearly doesn't feel in its own life, often coupled with an intense fear of what happens in public toilets.

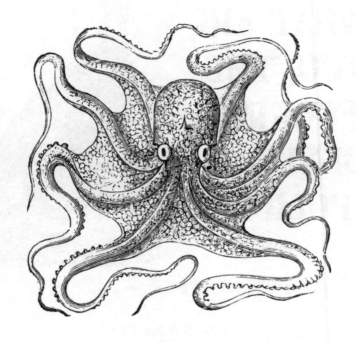

WELL, THIS IS FUCKING
AWKWARD

THAT IS SOME FUCKED-UP SHIT

STUNNED GUILLEMOT

At some point, these waterfowl just gave up trying to understand
the world around them.

HABITAT: Near Wi-Fi and a power outlet.

IDENTIFYING CHARACTERISTICS: Glassy-eyed, they acknowledge that we
are in a terrible hellscape and then continue to binge-watch Netflix.

OUR EXPECTATIONS FOR YOU WERE LOW, BUT HOLY FUCK

EVALUATIVE MERGANSER

This invasive species wraps itself in the protective cloak of 'constructive criticism' and 'feedback' but is more interested in point-scoring and its general feeling of superiority. Once there's an evaluative merganser on your management team, it's probably time to burn the whole thing down and start again.

HABITAT: Always in their office, and you have to come to them.

IDENTIFYING CHARACTERISTICS: A commitment to the numbers, because if they can make the numbers, who gives a shit about how they accomplished it?

TODAY'S GOLD
MEDAL FOR
BEING THE
STUPIDEST
GOES TO YOU

I BET THIS
PROBLEM
WILL GO AWAY
IF WE HAVE
MORE FUCKING
MEETINGS

GET OUT OF MY FUCKING FACE

IRATE STORK

These birds are associated with the delivery of babies in folklore, but in real life they should never be put anywhere near the extreme challenge to one's self-restraint known as a human child.

HABITAT: Frustratingly, these birds prefer to nest near the moat of the fairy-tale castle.

IDENTIFYING CHARACTERISTICS: Long legs and necks.

YOU ARE TESTING MY PATIENCE

WELCOME
TO HELL

ARE YOU FUCKING KIDDING ME?

WHO FUCKING CARES?

THIS SHIT AGAIN

YOU CAN ALL FUCK OFF UNTIL MONDAY

REASONABLE PIGEON

This bird walks the fine line between work–life balance and not giving a shit. Though if it gets all its work done, does it really matter?

HABITAT: Building Lego with the kids.

IDENTIFYING CHARACTERISTICS: The ability to disconnect from every contact method and vanish from its desk in the space between 16.52 and 17.00 p.m.

HOW ABOUT SOME FUCKING DECORUM

COURTEOUS DUCK

Policing your tone with no regard for its own, this duck is simply trying to derail you. Minute-to-minute reality does not apply; yesterday was 1,000 years ago in another era and all those people are dead now. Every word of every interaction is parsed in a vacuum. Context not only doesn't matter, it is actively shunned.

HABITAT: Wedged firmly in the middle of the pathetic, shouty mess that passes for political discourse these days.

IDENTIFYING CHARACTERISTICS: A tenuous grasp of grammar and punctuation combined with an unearned confidence that it is 'winning'.

LOOK AT ME NOT GIVING A SHIT

FULMINATING GREBE

Methinks the bird doth protest too much, or however that saying goes. The fulminating grebe loudly, defiantly proclaims that it does not care but then retreats to its nest to cry.

HABITAT: The Twitter mentions of people it had to seek out in order to read their opinions so they could not care about them.

IDENTIFYING CHARACTERISTICS: Loud voice, red-rimmed eyes, despair.

FUCK ALL YOU GUYS

INFELICITOUS DUCK

Known for inappropriately expressing its emotions, this duck cares strongly about its family and friends. No matter how often it tells you to fuck off, if you actually fucked off it would be heartbroken.

HABITAT: Wherever you are, telling you to fuck off.

IDENTIFYING CHARACTERISTICS: The infelicitous duck is very good at hugging. The hugs just come with inappropriate whispers in your ear.

SAYONARA, MOTHERFUCKERS

Acknowledgements

This book would not have been possible without the following people.

Nolan, Oliver, Theo and Vanessa: thank you for putting up with all of the terrible ideas that led to this good one. Vanessa, I'm sorry about the three-foot print that says 'EAT FARTS' on Nolan's wall. Nolan, I hope you like your print.

Carrie from the Audubon Society: your email changed everything.

Beth from Unbound: thank you for pushing me to do this.

Thomas Bewick: you are at the same time a great artist and also the grumpiest motherfucker who ever wrote a book about birds. You are an inspiration.

An extra-special thank you to the 1,600 Legendary Bird Friends whose support made this book possible.

A Note on the Author

Aaron Reynolds is a humorist, professional speaker and the man behind the @EffinBirds and @swear_trek Twitter accounts. When he's not on Twitter, you can find him producing a series of podcasts and at Comic-Cons dressed as George Lucas. He has been a baseball writer, a fine art printer and a mall Santa Claus photographer. Aaron was raised in Mississauga, Canada, a suburb where they cut down all the trees and named the streets after them. He currently splits his time between Toronto and Ottawa.

Unbound is the world's first crowdfunding publisher, established in 2011.

We believe that wonderful things can happen when you clear a path for people who share a passion. That's why we've built a platform that brings together readers and authors to crowdfund books they believe in – and give fresh ideas that don't fit the traditional mould the chance they deserve.

This book is in your hands because readers made it possible. Everyone who pledged their support is listed below. Join them by visiting unbound.com and supporting a book today.

Dan Ackroyd
Caitlin Emily Adams
Neale Adams
Marsha Adix
afuzzyllama
Iain Ager
Farah Ahmed
Tobias Aichele
Leslie Aiken
Norb Aikin

Liz Aitken
Jessica Aldrich
Bruce Alexander
Evan Alexander
Diane Allan
Mireille Allegre
Louise Allen
Mike Allen
Rachel Allen
Heather Allman

Matthew Almeida
Jody Ambrose
Gene Ammon
Angela Anderson
Ivy M. Anderson
Mairead Anderson
Tracy Anderson
Caron Andregg
Vanessa Andrews
Oleynik Andrey

anjatheTEAgirl

Katherine Anthony

Paul Antompietri

Paris Apostoloppulos

Elena Apostolos

Emily Applen

Hugh Arai

Rhiannon Archer

Ben Arellano Delgado

Argyll Productions

Simon Armstrong

Steven Armstrong

Angie Arnold

Bob Arnson

John Arnzen

C Arthur

Michael Asmussen

Blaise Aspden

Julie Atwood

Leslie Ault I

Tom Avalon

Sarah Avampato

The Avelis Family

Aren B

Constantin B

Scott Backer

Captain Badbeard

Christopher Bailey

Graham Bailey

Jon Bailey

Ze Baird Schutte

Erich Baker

Katie Baker

Miri Baker

William Baker

Rachel Balcombe

Cameron Bales

Kari Banta

Joel Banuelos

João Barbosa

Josie Barker

Adam Barkley

Lisa Barlow-Busch

Bryan Barnes

Marilyn Barney

Lee Barnum

Lydia Barram

David Barrett

Michael Barron

Stephen Barteaux

Matt Bartels

Robert Barten

Elizabeth Bassett

Mike Battle

Mike Bauman

Mairi Beacon

Jocelyn Beard

Sue Beard

Dan Beasley

Jeff Beaudoin

Cindy Beaulé

Christopher Beccia

Deborah Beckwin

Zaphod Beeblebrox

Conny Beinhofer

Nick Bell

Francesca Bellu

Nikki Belmonte

Their beloved horse

Lindsey Bembli

Sally Bence

Cathy @badassbookjockey Benge

Julie Bennack

Lee Benningfield

Aimee Benson

Carrie Benson

Francisco Bernasconi

Jillian Berninger

Simon Berry

Esther Bertram

Kathleen Betti

Alisa Beyninson

Toby Bianchi

Casey Bice

Christine Biela

Abra Bigham

Anna Bigland

Michael Bikovitsky

Tracey Birch

Birdman

Anita Bischoff

Keith Bitter

Jeff Black

Beth Blackwood

Steven Blake

Lucas Blank

Aaron Blankenship

Emily Blizzard

Matthew Bloch
Steve Blundell
Derrick Bodkin
@boejurt
Nathalie Boisard-
   Beudin
Andrew Bold
Gavin Bollinger-Brown
Shirley Bomgaars
Sonya Bond
Michelle E. Bondy
Michelle Emily Bondy
Jess Bongaarts
Melody Bonnette
Todd Bonzalez
Alex Booer
Josh Bost
Jay Bougie
Katelyn Bougie
Rachelle Bourdon
Lesley Bourke
Evan Bourns
Janie Boutwell
Laura Bouwman
Jeremy Bow
Jessica Bowers
Marshall Bowers
Nikki Bowman
Katie Boyd
Claire Boyles
Andy Boynton
Chris Braddock
Adam Bradley

Elizabeth Bradley
Jen Bradshaw
Libby Bradshaw
Drew and Lisa
   Bradstock
Ellie Brady
Kristina Braell
Josh Brand
Sarah Brand
Lisa Brank
Kathy Brantley
Asbjørn Brask
Merinda Brayfield
Duane Bredel
Andrea Bredemeyer
Brian Brennan
Clare Brennan
Jacinta Brennan
Norah Brennan
Chris Broadbent
Pauline Brock
Stuart Bromwich
Bradford Brooks
Jess Brooks
Kat Brophy
BrotherRock
Phillip Broughton
Allison Brown
Andrew Brown
Donna Brown
Herschel Brown
Jennifer Brown
Nicky Brown

Sarah Brown
Sheila Brown
Aaron Brox
Ed Bruce
Luis Bruno
Chris Brush
Romain Bruzzese
Kathy Bryant
Joel Buchanan
James Buckley
Lesley Budge
Anjela Bugher
Simon Bugler
Eugene Bukhtin
Rachel Burch
Matthew Burger
Trish Burger
Brendan Burke
Daisy Burnell
Brandi Burnett
Ali Burns
Christine Burns
Denise Burt
Joe Burt
Lucy Burton
Karen Bury
Bekky Bush
Michael Bushell
Sarah Butcher
Mikaela Butler
Billy D. Butt
Carolyn Buzby
Brenna Bychowski

Dave Byler
Meghan Byrum
C44
Brett Cabeca
Katharine Cagney
Debbie Cain
Matthew Cain
Corin Caliendo
Dave Camp
Ericka Camp
Diana Campbell
Margaret Campbell
Rebecca Campbell
Branta Canadensis
Laura Cantrell
L Careless
Matt Caris
Jessica Carlson
Ann Carrier
Joe Carter
Matthew Carter
Sonja Carter
Dawn Cartwright
Mike Casaday
Darren Castle
Alexandra Cat
Wendy Catalano
Ruth Cattell
Cerise Cauthron
Katie Cerar
David Chamberlain
Kathleen Chamberlain
Maggie Chambers

Eric Chamois
David Chang van
    Oordt
Amanda Changuris
Kate Chapman
Tulsa Chapter
Elizabeth Charlton
Patricia Chavez
Paul Chernoff
Greg Childs
Rick Chlopan
Kasper Christensen
Chloe Christenson
Lisa Church
Mike Ciccotti
Ann Cihon
Valerie Cimarossa
Brent Cizek
Keith Clark
Sue Clark
Lindsey Clarke
Louise Clarke
Tara Clarke-Fontana
Adria Clawson
Amelia E. Clegg
Gemma Clucas
Derek Cluck
Beth Coale
Angela Coburn
Sandra Coffta
Julia Colby
Anne Cole
Christopher Collins

Danielle Collins
Joe Compeau
Caitlin Compton
Alexander Conroy
Christopher Conroy
Louis Constandinos
Caleb Cook
Drewsy Cook
Amy Cooke
Chris Coomber and
    Kaylee O'Shea
Mark E Cooper
Elizabeth Copeland
Rebecca Coplon
Jed Corcoran
Lena Cornelis
Adrienne Cornwall
@corq
Kelly Cosgrove
Chris Cote
Christopher Cotta
L. Coues
Kyle K. Courtney
Julie Courtwright
Caroline Cowan
Martin Cowgill
Wes Cowley
Allison Cox
Catriona Cox
Mercedes Coyle
Kristen Crandell
Stephen Crane
Crazy ChiknLady

Mike Creighton
Cara Crisostomo
Bradley Crone
Marilyn Croser
David Crowe, Jr.
Anthony W Crunk
Crystal Element
Tom & Susan Cucuzza
John Cunningham
Melissa Cunningham
L Curtin
Luciana Custodio
Geri D
Nicole D
Peter D'Hoye
Jason D'Olier
Jordan D'Olier
Justin D'Olier
Tracy Dale
Jennifer Dameron
Sarah Dammyer
Judith Danewitz
John Danziger
Sruthi Dasika
Gwynneth Davidoff
Andrew Davies
Claire Davies
John Davies
Sarah Davin
Maureen Davis
Christine Davis-
    Keeney
Jeff Day

Julia de Cadenet
Roselle de Castro
Gerdien de Galan
Vanda de la Mata
James de Winter
Jordan Deasy
John Dedell
Valerie Delevan
Carole Dempsey
Jamie Dempster
Aaron Deraps
Paula Derickson
Dan Deschamps
Michele Desoer
Heather Desserud
Nicole Dettmar
Neil Dewhurst
Donald DeWolfe
Elizabeth Dhadwar
Scilla Di Donato
Matthew Dick
Karin Dickensheets
Claire Dickson
Shane Digiovanna
Toby Dignum
Carrie Dirk
Larry Dixon
Katherine Dobbins
Scott Dobson
Brooks Doherty
Kristine Doktor
Jane Dominowski
Colleen Donaldson

Donnicabab
Scott Douglas-Watson
Mareta Doyle
Meghan Drake
Linda Drennan
Maggie Dressel
Jennifer Dritt
Katy Driver
Rebekah Drury
Diana Dubinsky
Cynthia Dueltgen
Ole-Morten Duesund
Hannah Duff
Tom Duffin
Melanie Duffner
Emma Duke
Nathalie Dunbar
DG Duncan
Lizzy Dunfee
Fiona Dunham
Alex Dunlop
David C. Dunthorn
Sam Durham
Barry Dwyer
Maeve Dwyer
Roger Eads
Renee Eastman
Grant Edgerton
Claire Edginton
Devin Edwards
Effin' Bird Lover
Laura Egger
Heather Egland

J David Eisenberg

Jennie Eldridge

JoAnn Ellero

Amber Elliott

Joshua Ellis

Magen Ellis

Peter Ellis

Eloquent Science

Maureen Empfield

Femke Engelse

Leo Engers

Marianne England

Dave Enright

John Erickson

Tomas Eriksson

Christine Ertl

Stuart Etchells

Suzanne Etheridge

Christina Evans

Kate Evans

Robert Evans

Andy Evans & Von
    Thompson-Wynn

Austin Everson

Kate Eyler-Werve

Rebecca F.

Sarah Fader

Mary Fallis

Michelle Aileen Fallis

Jennie Faries

Michael Farley

Anne Farmer

Jamie Farquharson

Ann Farrington

Sarah Felmus

Amy Feltman

Amanda Fenniak

Shawna Ferguson

Carolyn Fiddler

Michael Fiegel

John Field

Kirk Fields

Lucy Fields

Nicole Finch

Allison Fingleton

Caroline Finlay

Arlene Finnigan

Barry Douglas Fisher

David Fisher

The Fishes

Caitlin Fitz Gerald

Gabrielle Fitzgibbon

Colin Fitzpatrick

Laurel Flechtner

Mark Fleckenstein

Alison Fleming

Deborah Fleming

Sara Fleming

Sarah Florer

Matthew Flowers

Dan Flye

Billy Flynn

Jason Flythe

FNHT

Kelly Foley

Jason Folkers

Baptiste Fontaine

Jennifer Foray

Sam Forbes

Stuart Forbes

Katee Forbis

Amelia Ford

Bradley Ford

Theresa Foster

Marjolaine Fournier

Jamie Fowler

Rian Fowler

Andrew Fox

Mary Fox

Ben Francis

Alexis Frangis

Doug Franklin

Milane Frantz

Heather Frase

The Freeloaders

Maureen Freeman

Patrick Freeman

Rob Freeman

Mary Beth Frezon

Jamie Friedemann

Lorenza Frigerio

Anthony Friscia

Staci Fritz

Sergio Frosini

Miriam Frost

Kate
    FuckOffWithThatShit

Sara Fuentes

Max Fulham

Steve Fuller
Tara Fulton
Andrew Funk
Alex Furmanski
furnhusch
Sarah Furr
Hazel Fyfe
Becci G-C
Fabrice Gabolde
Ann Marie Gage
Dr. Elaine Gallagher
Amy Gallichan
Katharine Ganly
Richard Gant
Renette Garbutt
Chris Garcia
Ann-Marie Gardner
Darren Garnier
Christine Garretson-
    Persans
Fatima Maria Garrido
    Enjamio
Helen M. Garth
Nev Garven
Stephen Garvey
Sam Gawith
Carolyn Geason
Jeremy Gebben
Amro Gebreel
James Genge
Jane George
Halley Georgeson
Fuzzy Gerdes

Ann German
Shawna Giancola
Mark Gibson
Shauna Gibson
John Gilbert
Maggie Gilbert
Nik Gilbert
Sophie Gilbert
Julie Gilbey
Ruth Gilhooley
Elisa Gillespie
Laurel Gillette
Laura Gilligan
Simon Gillings
Lisa Gilmour
Cathy Gleason
Vicki Gloak
Barry & Karen
    Gloomquist
Becky Glynn
Will Glynn
Samantha Godden-
    Chmielowicz
Noemi Godefroy
El Camino-driving
    Uncle Greg Goebel
    & Associates
#1 Uncle Dan Goebel
    & Associates, LLC
Elderly Uncle Jimmy
    Goebel &
    Associates, LLC
Paul Goff

Pamela Golden
Jane Goldman
Thorsten Goldschmidt
Caroline Goldsmith
Hksurfer Gonzales
Jessica Gonzalez
Jane Goodenough
Michael Goodfellow
Dustin Goodwin
Helen Gordon
David Gordon-
    Johnson
Ryan Gorman
Ian Gough
Jocelyn Gould
Jacob Grass
Laurie Gravell
Jillian Graves
Dennis Gray
David Green
Simon Green
Thomas Green
Anna Greenwood
Jann Greenwood
James Gregory-Monk
Julie Grewer
Judith Griffith
Emma Griffiths
Megan Griffiths
Stanley Griswold
Christine Grosvenor
Simon Groth
Victoria Grundle

Kevin Gubbins
Holly Guglielmetti
Aaron Guilmette
Dra. Silvia Guirola
Dawn Gulick
Angela Gunn
Sara Gurnett
Heidi Gustafson
Margaret Gustafson
Aerin Guy
gweiloeye
Layla "Azalea" H.
Alex Hacker
David Hahn
Robert Haines
Dominik Hajduk
Cathryn Adele Hall
Charlotte Haller
Rocky Halleron
Kate Halloran
Neill Halpin
Christopher Halsey
Juliet Hamak
Keith Hambling
Hallie Hamby
Jim Hamilton
Zeke Hamilton
Lauren Hammond
Jennifer Hamp
Erik Hanberg
Edward Hancox
Handsome Stranger
Kathryn Hansel

Kate and Betsy Hansen
Karyn Hantzmon
Happy Birthday 2019!
   - XO, B.E.
Mark Harbers
James Hardacre
Kat Hardaway
Matthew Hardeman
Joey Hardwick
Sam Hardy
Margo Hardyman
Joshua Harms
Kimberly Harp
Simon Harper
Eliot Harris
Therese Harris
Jill Harrison
Rachel Harrison
Mathew Hart
Amanda Harvey
Eleanor Harvey
Jessica Hately
David Hatten
Elle Havis
Charles Hawkins
Kathryn Hawkins
Katherine Haxton
Connie Heap
Maryanne Heard
Irwin Hébert
Emily and Jill Helms
Meridith Hemond
Dina Henrike

Loretta Henslick
Dennis Martin Herbers
Kiera Herbert
Joshua Hernandez
Laura Herr
Russ Herrold
Megan Hesselink
Karen Hester
Renee Hewitt
Tom Hickerson
Adam Hicks
David Hicks
Liza Hicks
Des Higgins
Stacy Hill
Stephanie Hill
Wendy Hill
Kim Hilliard
Robert Hillier
Maggie Hilt
Andrew Hinton
Greg Hitchcock
Alex Hitchins
Matt Hodges
Martin Hodgson
Susan Hodgson
Lysa Hoffman
Sara Hoffman
Manuela Hoffmann
Erin Hofmeister
Steve Hogarty
Michelle & Craig
   Holigroski

Haley Holiman
Dave Holland
Sarah Holliday
Lucy Hollwedel
Michelle Holshue
Wieteke Holthuijzen
Holly Hommerding
Honey Honey
Kelsey Hoover
Kelly Hopkins
Pamela Hopkins
Sarah Hopkins
Simon Horne
Bill Horsman
Karen Horton & Dani
    Coleman
Sarah Hotze
Erica Howard
Marian Howse
Franklin Hu
Shannon Hubbell
Leanne Huckaby
Michal Hughes
Antti Huhtamäki
Christy Hume
Annya Hundal
Brandon Hunt
Rowan Hunter
Chad Huntington
Laura Hutchings
Neal Huynh-Richard
Jordan Hynes
Insignificant Funds

Margaret Ippolito
Kelli Ireland
George Stanley Irving
Ron Irving
Elizabeth Israel-Davis
Dani J
Alesha Jackson
Amanda Jackson
Karen Jackson
Taliesin Jaffe
Jake Jakubek
H. Jameel al Khafiz
Jennifer James
Phoebe Janflone
Lee Jaschok
Karine Jegard
Alexander Jegtnes
Ben Jemmett
Joanna Jenkins
Jennanik
Tudor Jennings
Matthew Jensen
David Jensenius
Jay Jernigan
Neil Jerome
Cathy Jeske
Guillermo Jimenez
Michael Jimenez
Brendan Johnson
Dustin Johnson
Linnea Johnson
Emmy Maddy
Johnston

Michelle Johnston
Lorien Jollye
Ben Jones
Clare Jones
Dustan Jones
Jennifer Jones
Kris Jones
Laura Jones
Miriam Jones
Jacob Jones-Goldstein
jonhattan
Isabel Jordan
David Joyce
Phoebe Juel
Erika Kachama-Nkoy
tortilla kads
Teresa & Skuzz
    Kafentzis
Kaiju
Courtney Kansler
Lura Kaplan
Aamil Karimi
Chloe Karr
Stephanie Keahey
John Kearney
Kristin Keen
Laura Kehler
Laura Keith
Andy Kellett
Annemarie Kelly
George Kelly
Sian Kelly
Becca Kemp

John & Sarah Kent
El Kentaro
Mark Kerner
Jessica Kia
Evan Kidd
Dan Kieran
Caitlin Kight
Tamara Killion
Jennifer Kimball
Wendy Kinder
Paul & Amie
  Kinderflooglemeister
Elana King
Tabitha King
Ally Kingdon
Don Kingfield
Dave Kinghan
Kathy Kirkpatrick
Roman Kiselev
Julie Klassen
Ken Klavonic
Ann Klee
Angela Kleis
Sophie Klevenow
James Knight
Marie-Anne Knight
Diane Knights
Antonia Knoblich-
  Hirst
Deedee Knowit
Jean Knowles
Kevin Knudson
Dawn Koeller

Kathleen Koha
Jessica Kohn
Michael Kohne
Becky Kolakoski
Stacy Kolden
Amy Koliner
Jon Konst
Patrick Kontschak
Kalman Konyves
Adam Korengold
Anna Korula
Erin Kowalski
William Krause
Robert Kray
Carrie Krein
Dan Kreppein
Christine Krikorian
Kelly Kroese
Diana Krueger
Laura Kruse
Cecilia Kruszynski
Jessica Kuhlmey
Lisa Kupsh
Keren Kurtz
Jennifer Kussrow
Kristen Kwan
Robert Kwasniewski
Pierre L'Allier
Kim Ladin
M Laik
Robbie Laity
Girish Lalla
Grace Lambert-Smith

Jeanne Lambkin
Chelsey Lamoureux
Donna Lanclos
Jessica Landes
Corey Landstrom
Sheila Lane
Petet Larcombe
Ann Larimer
Adam Larsen
Helen Larson
Jess Larson
Phil & Becky Lashinski
Matthew Lathan
Kelly Lathrop
Anne Laurie
Laurie 18
Sarah Lawrence
Dan Lawson
Jeff Lawson
Kery Lawson
Dawn Leady
Petra Leahy
Kate Leary
Karen Leckey
Jacqueline Lee
Jessica Lee
Patrick Lee
Rob & Lauren Lee
Matt Lee (@mattl)
Derek LeLash
Carla Lennon
Phillip Leonard
Melissa Lerner

Angela Les
Katharina Lesk
Gaby Leuenberger
Kristen Lewis
Nita L. Lewis
Scott Liddell
Megan Liddell List
Jacki Liddle
Jonathan Lidgus
Rebecca Liedke
Joe Liedtke
Amanda Lien
Gail Lindekugel
Dustin Lindemann
Sandra Lindquist
Maddie Lindsey
Angie Lingk
Matt Linton
Kevin Liston
Tamasin Little
Deborah Lium
David Livingston
LizTRON
Andrew Local
Chris Lodge
Kit Loewen
Marion Logan
John & Christine
    Lomax
Basil Long
Gareth Long
Chloe Longley
Tom Loosemore

Renato Lopes
Valerie Lopez
Amanda Louden
Mike Loufus
John Loughlin
Jennie Louise
Sean Love
Gemma Lovegrove
Rachel Loveland
Matt Loveridge
David Lovitch
Catriona Low
Frani Lowe
Russell Lowe
Mindy Lowers
James Loxley
Suzanne Loyd
Dominic Luechinger
Michael Luffingham
Paul Luke
Timo Lüke
Jen Lutley
Naomi Luxford
Anna Lyaruu
Megan M
Jeff Mabon
Allison Macdonald
Karen Mace
Lauren MacGill
Edward MacGregor
Melissa Macias
Dean MacLanders
Shawn MacLean

James MacNutt
Deborah MacPherson
Agatha MacPie
Erin Madigan
Rebecca Mae
Lauren Magliola
Kumaran Mahalinga-
    Iyer
Mino Mahdi
Amber Mahoney
Walter Maier
Lisa Major
Kizzy Makinde
Corrick
Rosemarie Malanaphy
April Mallory
Carrie Malpica
Rich Malton
Heather Mandeville
Meghan Mann
Elliott Mannis
Christy March
Anne and Ryan
Marchand
Tiffany Marcheterre
Katie and Pete
Marchetto
Catherine Mardula
Berges Marie
Chris Marks
Chris Markuns
Andrew Marosok
Gib & Laura

Marquardt
Armando Marques
Amber Marrow-Jones
Alexis Marruffo
Julie Marschall
Stephanie Marsh
Brian Marshall
Hal Marshall
Paul Marshall
Alex Martin
Andrew Martin
Krista Martin
Robert Martin
SR Martin
Jan "endlife" Martinek
Samantha Maskill
Paula Mason
Robyn Masters
Kyle Matera
Martin Matheny
matsec
Ryan Matthews
Steve Matthews
Margot Maurer
maurezen
Peter Mavrikos
Mary Maxwell
Nik May
David Maystrovsky
Jen Mazalook
Zenia McAllister
Blair McBride
Iain McCafferty

Danielle McCament
Betsy McCann
Brian McCarthy
Lindsay McCarty
Patrick McColgan
Jesse McCollum
Scott McCombs
Ashley McConnell
Tara McCook
Eric McCormick
C McCurdy
Heather McDaid
Colleen McDaniel
Charlotte McDonald
Daniel McDonald
Debra McDonald
Teresa McDonold
Ian McDougall
Glen McFerren
Shey Mcfez
Peter McGinn
David McGuigan
Colin McGuire
Randy McIntosh
Andrew McIntyre
Colby McKague
Christopher McKay
Mairi McKay
Chris McKee
Neal McKegney
Kasey McKenna
Kristin McKenna
TJ McKenna

Rosie McKerr
James McLaren
Robin McLeod
Layla McMichael
Wendell McMurrain
Nick & Kim McNally
Georgia McNamara
Ben McNeely
Jamie McNeely
Calvin Mcphaul
Andrew McPherson
Leanna McPherson
SJ McQuillan
Kimberly McReynolds
Daniel Mead
Audrey Meade
Joel Meador
John Measures
Wendy Meehan
Ronald Mehring
Sarah Mei
Stephen Meister
Lizzy Llama Mellish
Cameron Mellor
Kerrin Mendler
Addie Metivier
Natalie Meyers
Mi'Lady
Randall Michael Jr
Michelle Michelbacher
Ali Middle
Ed Miles
Aaron Miller

Trever Miller
Catherine Mills
James Minot
Kacey Minton
Charlcye Mitchell
John Mitchell
Sara Mitchell
John Mitchinson
Andrew R. Mizener
Johanna Mizgala
Deena Mobbs
Laura Mobley
Jennifer Mock
Marc Molins
Russ Moll
Sarah Mongiat
Pantelis Monioudis
Nerwin D Monster
Hannah Moore
Jason Moore
Leslie E Moore
Nathan Moore
Andy Moorhouse
Noel Morales
Andy Moran
Steven Morgan
Ellen Morin
Tony Morley
Sally Morrison
Tina Morton
Stacy Moskal
Hannah Elizabeth
    Mountford

Deb Mrazik
MuellersKnife®
Mugu's Barb
Amanda Mullens
Sasha Müller
Sinead Mulready
Chris Murphy
Evelyn Murphy
Jaclyn Murphy
Julie Murphy
Kathryn Murphy
T Murray
Emily Murskyj
Kristina Muskiewicz
Matt Mutchler
Justin Myers
Myśka (Mrs Fox)
NastyCoCo
Rachel Naunton
Carlo Navato
Kelly Naylor
Karen Neko
Erin Nephin
Amanda Nerud
James Newman
Layla Newman
Sarah Newton-Scott
Renee "Snaredove"
    Nichol
Josh Nichols
Joey Nicholson
Kurt Nightingale
Jean Nisley

David Nix
Amanda Nixon
Kenya Nixon
JC Noble
Noel
Denise Noelle
Rob Nolen
Norfolk Bea
Error Notfound
Tracy O'Brien
Darren O'Connell
Dara O'Donnell
Sue O'Donnell
Rebecca O'Dwyer
Elizabeth O'Hara
James O'Hara
Kay O'Leary
Niamh O'Reilly
Ann O'Rourke
Karen O'Sullivan
Kevin O'Connor
Stéphanie Odegard
Lucinda Offer
Dustin Ogilvie
Raman Ohri
Nancy J Olds
    Magnotta
Kenna Olsen
Kat Olson
Lori Olson
Maggie Olson
Todd Olson
Tonje Olson

Rachel Olsson
Gregory Olver
Karen Olympia
Emily Oram
Jennifer Orlow
Ruth Ormston
Susana Orozco
Marina Oseeva
Vladislav Osmanov
Farallon Otter
Mark Otter
Doug Otto
Eric Ouellette
Nicole Ouwerkerk
Emily, Jon and Axl
    Owen
Ray Owen
Pam Owens
Genevieve Packer
Sara Page
Gerard Palmer
Carlos Tadeu Panato
    Junior
Glen Pappas
Karen Paquette
Jim Parberry
Bethany Parent
Lev Parikian
Israel Parreño
Chris Parry
Edward Parsons
Lia Pastorelli
Tania Patch

Trish Paton
Samantha Pattenden
Florian Patzl
Andrew Paulin
Noreen Pazderski
Roger Peachey
Angharad Bob Peacock
April Peacock
Sara Peak
Selina Pearson
Leah Peasley
Denis Pelletier
Roger Pence
Jo Penn
Jeremiah Perez
Rachel Perkins
Salimah Perkins
Neil Perry
Kevin Perttu
Denise Peterson
Erik Peterson
Michael Peterson
Phil Peterson
Scott Peterson
Charity A. Petrov
Alex Phillips
Stacy Phillips
Laurel Phoenix
Cadenza A. Piacere
Sarah Pickering Beers
Corinne Pierson
Mark Pilgrim
Joao Pimentel

pinkleton
Anthea Pitt
Wisconsin Platt
Ian Plenderleith
Michael Plunkett
Karmel Pohl
Valerie Polichar
Antoinette Polito
Claire Pollard
Justin Pollard
Mark Pomroy
Michele Poole
Raewyn Poole
Hal & Maria Potter,
    Jane Potter &
    Andrew Woods
Andy Poulastides
Andrew Pounce
Lindsay Powell
Matthew Praestgaard
Satadru Pramanik
Dale Pratt
Tracy Preston
Matt Price
Robert Prince
Beulah Prosser
Donald Proud
Joseph Provo
Sandra Prow
Zachary Prusak
Susi Quinn
Michelle Quinton
Lucy Radford

Mary Elaine Radford
Scott Rae
Sean Raffey
Kellie Rahija
Kimi Räikkönen
Tiina Rajasalo
Martin Ramsay
Deb Rasmussen
Hannah Rasmussen
Rebecca Raven
Kristine Rayburn
Sarah Raywood-
    Priestly
Sara Rebennack
Jason Ree
Kevin Reed
Nick Reeve
Kate Reeves
Naomi Reeves
Stuart Reeves
Alex Reid
Heather Reid-Murray
Joel Rein
Dr. Thomas Reinert
Nolan Reisbeck
#2 Uncle Jay Rempfer
    & Associates, LLC
Nick Renaud
Ann Renken
Tim Renner
Lilly Reynolds
Electra Rhodes
Victor Ricchezza

Elisa Richard
Adrienne Richardson
Rochelle Richardson &
    David Grasseschi
Laurie Richlovsky
Loralee Richter
Bri Riggio
Kristine Riley
Heather Ringman
Amy Ringuette
David Rintoul
Laura Ritchie
Susan J.E. Ritta
Matthew Ritter
Joanna Rives
Suzanne Robbins
Andrew Roberts
Joy Roberts
Wyn Roberts
Lee Robinson
Steven Roby and
    Laura Thomas
RockAleCakeMetalPie
Liliana Rodriguez
Keely Roen
Matthew Rofrano
Annie Rogers
Christopher Blake
    Rogers
Julia Rohs
Heather Rollins
Jennifer Romig
Michael Rose

Nathaniel Rose
Jamie Roselius
Paul Rosier
Craig Ross
Peter Ross
Catherine Rossi
M Rossi
Francois Rossouw
Teresa Rothaar
Jim Round
Colleen Royer
Russell Rubrecht
Thomas Ruddle
Christine Rudisill
Vickie Ruggiero
Laurel Ruma
A Rüscher
Michael Russell
Rhonds Rutherford
Deb Ryan
Danielle S
Lila Sadkin
Matthew Sadorf
Maggie Saffioti
Lily Sagers
Allison Salas
Lisa Salas
John Salazar
Jonathan Salisbury
Rodrigo B. Salvador
Jane Salvatori
Michael Salvia
Aaron Samuel

Erika Sanders
Janet Sanderson
Adam Santangelo
Dana Saretsky
Jennifer Sargent
Caitlin Sartin
Alicia Sasser
Major Satire
Anita Sauer
Paul Sauer
Robert Saunders
Susan Savia
Geoff Sawtell
Neil Sayer
Lisa Scanlon
ScarletSpitfire
Scott Schaffer
Whitney Scharer
Sam Schechter
Nicole Scherer
Julie Schlak
Liz Schlegel
S. K. Schnably
Chad Schrock
Diane Schultz
Amanda Schuster
Angela Schutt
Jamie Schwalbach
Andrew Schwartz
Jennifer Schwartz
Charles Schwope
Renza Scibilia
Anne-Marie Scott

Betsy Scroggs
Kirschen Seah
Michelle Seberras
Jeremy Secaur
Roseanne Segovia
Rosanne Seguin
Monica Segura
Lisa Seifert
Alyssa Selbrede
Megan Sellick
Matt Sellick & Marg
    McKee
Eliza Sells
Catherine Sevcenko
Robert Sexton
Beka Shafer
Nuha Shaikh
Polly Shanahan
Sophie Shanahan-
    Kluth
Laurence Shapiro
Heather Sharp
Cathleen Shattuck
Coral Sheldon-Hess
Aunty Shell
Gillian Shields
Claire & Matt
    Shomphe
Megan Sibbert
Rebecca Sickinger
Claire Siddle
Jamie Siglar
Francisco Silva

Pepe Silvia
Andrew Simchik
Alick Simmons
Naphtali Simonowits
Diana Simpson
Erin Simpson
Valerie Sinex
David Singletary
Austin Sipes
Louis Sisneros
Bruno Sista
SisterRainbow
Suzanne Skadowski
Rob @Skeddy Sked
Jonathan Slater
Christine Slaughter
Keith Sleight
Steven Sloan
Jaydot Sloane
Xander Smalbil
Alex Smith
Andrea Smith
Clayton Smith
Dan Smith
Frank Smith
Immy Smith
Jennifer Smith
Jules Smith
Kathy Smith
Lucy Smith
Martin Smith
Michael Smith
Sandra Smith

Greg Snook
Geoff Snowman
Sehar Sohail
Alexandru Şorodoc
Matthew Soucoup
Matthew Soucy
Melanie Southard
Steve Southart
Kathrina Southwell
Erik Sowa
Matthew Sowden
Alyn Sparkes
Shane Spencer
Katie Spicer
Todd Spigener
Ilona Spiro
Maxime St-Arneault
Anna St-Onge
Jen St. Louis
Peter St. Marie
Heather Stanavitch
Ruth Stanley
Katie Stansfield
Mark Stears
David Steele
Emily Steer
Nigel Steggel
Kurt Stein
Patrick Stepanian
Richard Stephens
Graham Stephenson
Heidi Sternberg
Oliver Stevens

Beau Steward
Kimberly Nicole
	Carroll Steward
Ian Stewart
Sara Stewart
Sandy Stith
Kennedy Stock
Ross Stockwell
Susanne Stohr
Jessica Stokes
Michelle "Turbo"
	Stokes
Professor Elizabeth
	Stokoe
Ariel Stone
James Stone
Nevan Stone
Adam Story
Katrina Stovold
Nikki Stoyko
Nancy Stracener
Marie-Michelle Strah
Katherine Straley
Long live Stringy Bob
Brendan Strong
Jack-Daniyel Strong
Sarah Struthers
Ashley Stueck
Sharad Stump
Kelly Sturken
Dan Sugalski
Bart Suichies
Margaret Sullivan

Lady Sumarumi
Celeste Summers
Rock Sumner
Chris Suslowicz
Daniel Sutcliffe
Immie Sutherland!
Keith Sutherland
Caroline Swan
Derek Swanson
Derek Sweet
Erik Swenson
Helen Szigeti
Jon Szymaniak
Kim T
Autumn Taddicken
Sahil C Tah, MD
Rusty Tailpiper
Tala
Sandra Tamkin
Taka Tanaka
Abby Tanner
Angela Tant
Sarah Tarnopolsky
Marie-Lan Taÿ Pamart
Gabrielle Taylor
Crystal Taylor-Papps
Tee Tee
Sandra Tekmen
Piper Terry
Jodi Tharan
Helena Thomas
Jan Thomas
Jeanna Thomas

Kiera Thomas
Amanda Thompson
Ginger Thompson
Julia Thompson
Meredith Thompson
Sydney Thompson
Melissa Thornton
David Thurston
Ella Tiarks
D Tobias
Laura Tomaja
James Tomkins
Chris Tomlinson
Matt Toth
Mai-Liis Tou
Chloe Tough
Elizabeth Towne
Alex Townsend
Zach Tracy
Alison Traweek
Paul M. Tredick
Jonathan Treml
Michelle Tribe
Carlo Trimarchi
Michaeleen Trimarchi
Stephanie Trimboli
Charles Trittin
Emma Trone
Chelsea Troy
Victoria Trudeau
Elizabeth
    Trzebiatowski
Kire Tsukiko

Jennifer Tubbs
Lee Tucker
Julianne Ture
Heather Turnbull
Sandra Turner
Pearce Turpin
Kristy Tye
Sharon & Andrew
    Tymens
Sharon Uliana
Laetitia Ulick
Finn Upham
Lindsey Valdivia
Laura Valentine
Lorraine Valestuk
Anna Valsami
Marieke Valstar
Andrea Valvassori
Martin Van Aken
Martijn van Dam
Gaby van Gaans
Will van Gulik -
    AS2613
Nikki Vane
Lindsey Vath
Becky Vaughan
Kevin Veloso
Pasquale Marco Veltri
Phil Venables
Fabio Venni
Matthew Vernon
Linda Verstraten &
    Pyter Wagenaar

Josh Vertolli
Andrew Vessey
Nicole Vickers & Ian
    Vickers
Annamarie Vickers &
    Stephan Jantz
Nicolas Vignon
John Vincent
Michelle Vincent
Spenser Vines
Jon Vranek
Giles Wade
Essie Wagner
Meagan Louise
    Wagoner
Susan Wainscott
Mickenzie Walbridge
Craig Walker
Martin Walker
Steve Walker
Dj Walker-Morgan
Cathy Wallace
Donald Wallace
David Wallensky
Liz Walsh
Matt Walsh
Shaun Walsh
Scott Walter
Karen Walton
Karen Walton
Natalie J. Ward
Nate Warfield
    (@n0x08)

Melissa Washburn
Joe Wass
Taylor Watford
Aja Watson
Angela Watson
Nichole Watson
Julie Watt
Kerrie Watts
Julie Weber-Roark
Sebastian Wegener
Chris Weigert
Andrew Weisburd
Hillary Weisman
Jennifer Weiss
Clare Wells
Sarah-Louise Wells
Tabor Wells
Anne Welsh
Emily Wenberg
Eileen Wennekers
Elizabeth West
Fiona West
Jennifer Westfall
Samuel Westwood
Katy Wheatley
Shawn Wheatley
Laura Wheatman
Helen Wheelock
James White
Stephen White
Susan White
The White One and
   the Dark One

Loren Whiteside
Don Whiteside™
Mike Whitfield
Lisa Whittingham
Lynne Whittle
Eric Wiener
Jeanne Wiener
Andrea Wiggins
Adam Wilk
Rhys Wilkins
Jules Wilkinson
Paul Wilks
Paul Willett
Cliff Williams
Eric Williams
Gareth Williams
Jaime Williams
Kate Williams
Nate Williams
Peter Williams
Catherine Williamson
Elizabeth Williamson
Eric Williamson
Todd Williamson
Angela Willis
Lew Willis
Andy Wilson
Debra Wilson
Kate Wilson
Natalie Wilson
Tamsin Wilson
Virginia Wilson
Zoe Wilson

Takel Windfeather
Ellen Wingenter
Sarah Winnicki
Liana Winsauer
Robert Winterhalter
To my friend, Megan
   Winton
Elizabeth Wisker
Cassie Withey-Rila
Shelley Witte
Melissa Wolf
Rose Wolf
Jen Woltemade
Yi Wen Wong
Antony Wood
Michelle Woodberry
Val Woodhouse
Matthew Woodman
Teagan Woods & Amy
   Kennedy
Matthew Woody
Joni Wooldridge
Teri Worthington
Alison Wraight
MaryRose Wright
Russell Wright
Mandy Wultsch
Bryan Wyatt
Maria Xilouri
Eddie Yasi
Heather Yates
Meredith Yayanos
Deb Yemenijian

David Yetter
Jennifer Yocum
Heather York
Amy Yost
Eli Young
Lori Young
Michelle Young
Sandra Young
Beth Younger

Susan Yount
Tamara Yunker
Yvette
Carl Zahrt
Michael & Marge
  Zakalik
Andrew EatMe
  Zamore
Zan and Doug

Chadwick Ziemer
Lena Zinuticz
Canneau Zoodles